Contents

Celebrations

Wisdom will multiply your days
and add years to your life.

Proverbs 9:11 (NLT)

Helen Steiner Rice

A New Year Brings
a New Beginning

As the New Year starts and the old year ends
There's no better time to make amends
For all the things we sincerely regret
And wish in our hearts we could somehow forget—
We all make mistakes, for it's human to err,
But no one need ever give up in despair,
For God gives us all a brand-new beginning,
A chance to start over and repent of our sinning—
And when God forgives us we, too, must forgive
And resolve to do better each day that we live
By constantly trying to be like Him more nearly
And to trust in His wisdom
and love Him more dearly—
Assured that we're never out of His care
And we're always welcome to seek Him in prayer.

A New Year!
A New Day!
A New Life!

Not only on New Year's but all the year through
God gives us a chance to begin life anew,
For each day at dawning we have but to pray
That all the mistakes that we made yesterday
Will be blotted out and forgiven by grace,
For God in His love will completely efface
All that is past and He'll grant a new start
To all who are truly repentant at heart.

❧

Helen Steiner Rice

Springtime Glory

∽

Flowers buried beneath the snow
Awakening again to live and grow-
Leaves that fell to the earth to die
Enriching the soil in which they lie-
Lifeless-looking, stark, stripped trees
Bursting with buds in the springtime breeze
Are just a few examples of
The greatness of God's power and love,
And in this blaze of springtime glory,
Just who could doubt in the Easter story!

∽

The Miracle of Christmas

The wonderment in a small child's eyes,
The ageless awe in the Christmas skies,
That nameless joy that fills the air,
The throngs that kneel in praise and prayer. . .
These are the things that make us know
That men may come and men may go,
But none will ever find a way
To banish Christ from Christmas Day. . .
For with each child there's born again
A mystery that baffles men.

Helen Steiner Rice

A Birthday Is a Gateway

A birthday is a gateway
Between old years and new,
Just an opening to the future
Where we get a wider view.
For it takes a lot of birthdays
To make us wise and kind
And to help us judge all people
With our heart and not our mind.
Every year brings new dimensions
That enable us to see
All things within a kinder light
And more perceptively.
So birthdays are the gateway
To what the future holds
And to greater understanding
As the story of life unfolds.

Inspiration for Daily Living

The Lord himself goes before you and will be
with you; he will never leave you nor forsake you.
Do not be afraid; do not be discouraged.

Deuteronomy 31:8 (NIV)

Helen Steiner Rice

Daily Inspiration

⁓

Special poems for special seasons
are meaningful indeed,
But daily inspiration is still man's greatest need.
For day by day all through the year,
not just on holidays,
Man should glorify the Lord in
deeds and words of praise.
And when the heart is heavy and
everything goes wrong,
May these daily words for daily needs
be like a cheery song
Assuring you He loves you and
that you never walk alone,
For in God's all-wise wisdom
your every need is known!

⁓

Showers of Blessings

Each day there are showers of
blessings sent from the Father above,
For God is a great, lavish giver,
and there is no end to His love. . .
And His grace is more than sufficient,
His mercy is boundless and deep,
And His infinite blessings are countless—
and all this we're given to keep
If we but seek God and find Him
and ask for a bounteous measure
Of this wholly immeasurable offering
from God's inexhaustible treasure. . .
For no matter how big man's dreams are,
God's blessings are infinitely more,
For always God's giving is greater
than what man is asking for.

Helen Steiner Rice

The Blessings of Patience and Comfort

Realizing my helplessness,
I'm asking God if He will bless
The thoughts you think and all you do
So these dark hours you're passing through
Will lose their grave anxiety
And only deep tranquility
Will fill your mind and help impart
New strength and courage to your heart.
So take the Savior's loving hand
And do not try to understand—
Just let Him lead you where He will,
Through pastures green and waters still,
And though the way ahead seems steep,
Be not afraid for He will keep
Tender watch through night and day,
And He will hear each prayer you pray.

Sweet Blessings

ⸯ

Wishing God's sweet blessings
Not in droplets but a shower,
To fall on you throughout the day
And brighten every hour.

ⸯ

Gifts from God

ⸯ

This brings you a million good wishes and more
For the things you cannot buy in a store—
Like faith to sustain you in times of trial,
A joy-filled heart and a happy smile,
Contentment, inner peace, and love—
All priceless gifts from God above!

ⸯ

Helen Steiner Rice

Blessings Devised by God

God speaks to us in many ways,
Altering our lives, our plans, and our days,
And His blessings come in many guises
That He alone in love devises,
And sorrow, which we dread so much,
Can bring a very healing touch. . .
For when we fail to heed His voice
We leave the Lord no other choice
Except to use a firm, stern hand
To make us know He's in command. . .
For on the wings of loss and pain,
The peace we often sought in vain
Will come to us with sweet surprise,
For God is merciful and wise. . .
And through dark hours of tribulation
God gives us time for meditation,
And nothing can be counted loss
Which teaches us to bear our cross.

Not by Chance or Happenstance

Into our lives come many things
to break the dull routine—
The things we had not planned
or that happen unforeseen—
The sudden, unplanned meeting that
comes with sweet surprise
And lights the heart with happiness
like a rainbow in the skies.
Now some folks call it fickle fate
and some folks call it chance,
While others just accept it
as a pleasant happenstance.
But no matter what you call it,
it didn't come without design,
For all our lives are fashioned
by the hand that is divine
And every lucky happening and every lucky break
Are little gifts from God above
that are ours to freely take.

Helen Steiner Rice

Beyond Our Asking

More than hearts can imagine
or minds comprehend,
God's bountiful gifts are ours without end.
We ask for a cupful when the vast sea is ours,
We pick a small rosebud from a garden of flowers,
We reach for a sunbeam but the sun still abides,
We draw one short breath but
there's air on all sides.
Whatever we ask for falls short of God's giving,
For His greatness exceeds every facet of living,
And always God's ready and eager and willing
To pour out His mercy, completely fulfilling
All of man's needs for peace, joy, and rest,
For God gives His children whatever is best.
Just give Him a chance to open His treasures,
And He'll fill your life with
unfathomable pleasures—
Pleasures that never grow worn out and faded
And leave us depleted, disillusioned, and jaded—
For God has a storehouse just filled to the brim
With all that man needs, if we'll only ask Him.

A Sure Way to
a Happy Day

Happiness is something we create in our minds—
It's not something you search for
And so seldom find.
It's just waking up and beginning the day
By counting our blessings and kneeling to pray.
It's giving up thoughts that breed discontent
And accepting what comes as a gift heaven-sent.
It's giving up wishing for things we have not
And making the best of whatever we've got.
It's knowing that life is determined for us
And pursuing our tasks
Without fret, fume, or fuss. . .
For it's by completing what God gives us to do
That we find real contentment and happiness, too.

Helen Steiner Rice

A Thankful Heart

Take nothing for granted, for whenever you do,
The joy of enjoying is lessened for you.
For we rob our own lives much more than we know
when we fail to respond or in any way show
Our thanks for the blessings that daily are ours—
The warmth of the sun, the fragrance of flowers,
The beauty of twilight, the freshness of dawn,
The coolness of dew on a green velvet lawn,
The kind little deeds so thoughtfully done,
The favors of friends and the love that someone
Unselfishly gives us in myriad ways,
Expecting no payment and no words of praise.
Oh, great is our loss when we no longer find
A thankful response to things of this kind.
For the joy of enjoying and the fullness of living
Are found in the heart
that is filled with thanksgiving.

Things to Be Thankful For

∽

The good, green earth beneath our feet,
The air we breathe, the food we eat,
Some work to do, a goal to win,
A hidden longing deep within
That spurs us on to bigger things
And helps us meet what each day brings—
All these things and many more
Are things we should be thankful for. . .
And most of all, our thankful prayers
Should rise to God because He cares.

∽

Helen Steiner Rice

Words to Live By

We all need words to live by,
To inspire us and guide us,
Words to give us courage
When the trials of life betide us.
And the words that never fail us
Are the words of God above,
Words of comfort and of courage
Filled with wisdom and with love.

Words of Encouragement

Your word is a lamp to my feet
And a light to my path.

Psalm 119:105 (NKJV)

Helen Steiner Rice

Do Not Be Anxious

Do not be anxious, said our Lord,
Have peace from day to day—
The lilies neither toil nor spin,
Yet none are clothed as they.
The meadowlark with sweetest song
Fears not for bread or nest
Because he trusts our Father's love
And God knows what is best.

Never Be Discouraged

There is really nothing we need know
or even try to understand
If we refuse to be discouraged
and trust God's guiding hand,
So take heart and meet each minute
with faith in God's great love,
Aware that every day of life
is controlled by God above
And never dread tomorrow
or what the future brings
Just pray for strength and courage
and trust God in all things,
And never grow discouraged—
be patient and just wait,
For God never comes too early,
and He never comes too late.

Helen Steiner Rice

No Room for Blessings

Refuse to be discouraged—
refuse to be distressed,
For when we are despondent,
our lives cannot be blessed.
Doubt and fear and worry close
the door to faith and prayer,
And there's no room for blessings
when we're lost in deep despair.
So remember when you're troubled
with uncertainty and doubt,
It is best to tell our Father
what our fear is all about.
For unless we seek His guidance
when troubled times arise,
We are bound to make decisions
that are twisted and unwise.
But when we view our problems
through the eyes of God above,
Misfortunes turn to blessings
and hatred turns to love.

Blessings Come in Many Guises

When troubles come and things go wrong
And days are cheerless and nights are long,
We find it so easy to give in to despair
By magnifying the burdens we bear.
We add to our worries by refusing to try
To look for the rainbow in an overcast sky,
And the blessings God sent in a darkened disguise
Our troubled hearts fail to recognize,
Not knowing God sent it not to distress us
But to strengthen our faith and redeem us and bless us.

Helen Steiner Rice

There Are Blessings
in Everything

Blessings come in many guises
That God alone in love devises,
And sickness, which we dread so much,
Can bring a very healing touch,
For often on the wings of pain
The peace we sought before in vain
Will come to us with sweet surprise,
For God is merciful and wise. . .
And through long hours of tribulation
God gives us time for meditation,
And no sickness can be counted loss
That teaches us to bear our cross.

Never Despair,
God's Always There

In sickness or health,
In suffering and pain,
In storm-laden skies,
In sunshine and rain,
God always is there
To lighten your way
And lead you through darkness
To a much brighter day.

*

Helen Steiner Rice

It's a Wonderful World

In spite of the fact we complain and lament
And view this old world with much discontent,
Deploring conditions and grumbling because
There's so much injustice and so many flaws,
It's a wonderful world, and it's people like you
Who make it that way by the things that they do.
For a warm, ready smile or a kind, thoughtful deed
Or a hand outstretched in an hour of need
Can change our whole outlook
and make the world bright
Where a minute before just nothing seemed right.
It's a wonderful world and it always will be
If we keep our eyes open and focused to see
The wonderful things we are capable of
When we open our hearts to God and His love.

Words of Comfort

All praise to God, the Father of our Lord
Jesus Christ. God is our merciful Father
and the source of all comfort.

2 Corinthians 1:3 (NLT)

Helen Steiner Rice

God Bless and Keep You in His Care

There are many things in life
we cannot understand,
But we must trust God's judgment
and be guided by His hand. . .
And all who have God's blessing
can rest safely in His care,
For He promises safe passage on
the wings of faith and prayer.

God's Tender Care

When trouble comes, as it does to us all
God is so great and we are so small—
But there is nothing that we need know
If we have faith that wherever we go
God will be waiting to help us bear
Our pain and sorrow, our suffering and care—
For no pain or suffering is ever too much
To yield itself to God's merciful touch!

God's Keeping

To be in God's keeping is surely a blessing,
For though life is often dark and distressing,
No day is too dark and no burden too great
That God in His love cannot penetrate.

Helen Steiner Rice

There's Peace and Calm in the Twenty-third Psalm

With the Lord as your Shepherd
you have all that you need,
For if you follow in His footsteps
wherever He may lead,
He will guard and guide and keep you
in His loving, watchful care,
And when traveling in dark valleys,
your Shepherd will be there. . .
His goodness is unfailing,
His kindness knows no end,
For the Lord is a Good Shepherd
on whom you can depend. . .
So when your heart is troubled,
you'll find quiet, peace, and calm
If you'll open up the Bible and
just read this treasured psalm.

There Is a Reason for Everything

God never hurts us needlessly
and He never wastes our pain;
For every loss He sends to us
is followed by rich gain.
And when we count the blessings
that God has so freely sent,
We will find no cause for murmuring
and no time to lament.
For our Father loves His children
and to Him all things are plain;
He never sends us pleasure when
the soul's deep need is pain.
So whenever we are troubled
and when everything goes wrong,
It is just God working in us
to make our spirits strong.

Helen Steiner Rice

It Takes the Bitter and Sweet

Life is a mixture of sunshine and rain,
Laughter and teardrops, pleasure and pain,
Low tides and high tides, mountains and plains,
Triumphs, defeats, and losses and gains,
But always in all ways or some dread affliction,
Be assured that it comes with
God's kind benediction,
And if we accept it as a gift of His love,
We'll be showered with blessings
from our Father above.

Somebody Cares

⁓

Somebody cares and always will—
The world forgets, but God loves you still.
You cannot go beyond His love
No matter what you're guilty of,
For God forgives until the end—
He is your faithful, loyal friend. . .
And though you try to hide your face,
There is no shelter anyplace
That can escape His watchful eye,
For on the earth and in the sky
He's ever-present and always there
To take you in His tender care
And bind the wounds and mend the breaks
When all the world around forsakes.
Somebody cares and loves you still,
And God is the Someone who always will.

⁓

Helen Steiner Rice

God Will Not Fail You

When life seems empty and there's no place to go,
When your heart is troubled
and your spirits are low,
When friends seem few and nobody cares—
There is always God to hear your prayers. . .
And whatever you're facing will seem much less
When you go to God and confide and confess,
For the burden that seems too heavy to bear
God lifts away on the wings of prayer. . .
And seen through God's eyes
earthly troubles diminish,
And we're given new strength to face and to finish
Life's daily tasks as they come along
If we pray for strength to keep us strong. . .
So go to our Father when troubles assail you,
For His grace is sufficient and He'll never fail you.

Never Alone

Since fear and dread and worry
Cannot help in any way,
It's much healthier and happier
To be cheerful every day—
And if we'll only try it
We will find, without a doubt,
A cheerful attitude's something
No one should be without—
For when the heart is cheerful
It cannot be filled with fear,
And without fear the way ahead
Seems more distinct and clear—
And we realize there's nothing
We need ever face alone,
For our heavenly Father loves us
And our problems are His own.

Helen Steiner Rice

Eagles' Wings

How little we know what God has in store
As daily He blesses our lives more and more.
I've lived many years and learned many things,
But today I have grown new spiritual wings,
For pain has a way of broadening our view
And bringing us closer in sympathy, too,
To those who are living in constant pain
And trying somehow to bravely sustain
The faith and endurance to keep on trying
When they'd almost welcome the peace of dying.
And without this experience
I would have lived and died
Without fathoming the pain of Christ crucified,
For none of us know what pain's all about
Until our spiritual wings start to sprout.
So thank You, God, for the gift You sent
To teach me that pain is heaven-sent.

Words of Challenge

I can do all things through Christ
who strengthens me
Philippians 4:13 (NKJV)

Helen Steiner Rice

Take Time to Appreciate God's Blessings

Blessings are all around us.
If we look we can recognize a blessing in
each day, each hour, each minute,
each family member, each friend, each neighbor,
each community, each city, each nation,
each challenge, each word of encouragement,
each flower, each sunbeam, each raindrop,
each awesome wonder crafted by God,
each star, each sea, each bird, each tree,
each sorrow, each disappointment,
each faith, each prayer.

✐

Be Glad

Be glad that your life has been full and complete,
Be glad that you've tasted the bitter and sweet.
Be glad that you've walked in sunshine and rain,
Be glad that you've felt both pleasure and pain.
Be glad that you've had such a full, happy life,
Be glad for your joy as well as your strife.
Be glad that you've walked with courage each day,
Be glad you've had strength for each step of the way.
Be glad for the comfort that you've found in prayer.
Be glad for God's blessings, His love, and His care.

Helen Steiner Rice

Take Time to Be Kind

Kindness is a virtue given by the Lord—
It pays dividends in happiness and joy is its reward.
For if you practice kindness in all you say and do,
The Lord will wrap His kindness
around your heart and you.

Look Up

It's easy to grow downhearted
when nothing goes your way,
It's easy to be discouraged
when you have a troublesome day,
But trouble is only a challenge
to spur you on to achieve
The best that God has to offer
if you have the faith to believe!

Not What You Want but What God Wants

Do you want what you want when you want it?
Do you pray and expect a reply?
And when it's not instantly answered
Do you feel that God passed you by?
Well, prayers that are prayed in this manner
Are really not prayers at all,
For you can't go to God in a hurry
And expect Him to answer your call.
For prayers are not meant for obtaining
What we selfishly wish to acquire,
For God in His wisdom refuses
The things that we wrongly desire. . .
Wake up! You are missing completely
The reason and purpose of prayer,
Which is really to keep us contented
That God holds us safe in His care.
And God only answers our pleadings
When He knows that our wants fill a need,
And whenever our will becomes His will,
There is no prayer that God does not heed!

ॐ

Helen Steiner Rice

The Peace We're Seeking

If we but had the eyes to see
God's face in every cloud,
If we but had the ears to hear
His voice above the crowd;
If we could feel His gentle touch
In every springtime breeze
And find a haven in His arms
'Neath sheltering, leafy trees. . .
If we could just lift up our hearts
Like flowers to the sun
And trust His loving promise
And pray, "Thy will be done,"
We'd find the peace we're seeking,
The kind no man can give,
The peace that comes from knowing
He died so we might live!

Faith, Not Feeling

When everything is pleasant and bright
And the things we do turn out just right,
We feel without question that God is real,
For when we are happy, how good we feel. . .
But when the tides turn and gone is the song
And misfortune comes and our plans go wrong,
Doubt creeps in and we start to wonder,
And our thoughts about God are torn asunder—
For we feel deserted in time of deep stress,
Without God's presence to assure us and bless. . .
And it is then when our senses are reeling
We realize clearly it's faith and not feeling—
For it takes great faith to patiently wait,
Believing God comes not too soon or too late.

Helen Steiner Rice

Three Treasures

There are three treasures
More priceless than gold.
For if you possess them
You've riches untold—
For with faith to believe
What your eyes cannot see,
And hope to look forward
To joy yet to be,
And love to transform
The most commonplace
Into beauty and kindness
And goodness and grace,
There's nothing too much
To accomplish or do.
For with faith, hope, and love
To carry you through,
Your life will be happy
And full and complete.
For with faith, hope, and love
The bitter turns sweet.

The Seasons
of Life

There is a time for everything,
and a season for every activity under the heavens.
Ecclesiastes 3:1 (NIV)

Helen Steiner Rice

The Blessings of God's Seasons

We know we must pass through the seasons God sends,
Content in the knowledge that everything ends,
And oh, what a blessing to know there are reasons
And to find that our souls must, too,
have their seasons—
Bounteous seasons and barren ones, too,
Times for rejoicing and times to be blue—
But meeting these seasons of dark desolation
With the strength that is born of anticipation
Comes from knowing that every season of sadness
Will surely be followed by a springtime of gladness.

⁓

Growing Older Is Part of God's Plan

You can't hold back the dawn
or stop the tides from flowing
Or keep a rose from withering
or still a wind that's blowing—
And time cannot be halted
in its swift and endless flight,
For age is sure to follow youth
like day comes after night. . .
For He who sets our span of years
and watches from above
Replaces youth and beauty
with peace and truth and love—
And then our souls are privileged
to see a hidden treasure
That in youth escapes our eyes
in our pursuit of pleasure. . .
So passing years are but blessings
that open up the way
To the everlasting beauty of God's eternal day.

Helen Steiner Rice

The Happiness You Already Have

Memories are treasures
that time cannot destroy;
They are the happy pathway
to yesterday's bright joy.

❧

With Him Forever

❧

The waking earth in springtime
Reminds us it is true
That nothing really ever dies
That will not rise anew. . .
So trust God's all-wise wisdom
And doubt the Father never,
For in His heavenly Kingdom
You'll live with Him forever.

❧

Life's Golden Autumn

Memory opens wide the door on a happy day like this,
And with a sweet nostalgia we longingly recall
The happy days of long ago that seem the best of all. . .
But time cannot be halted
in its swift and endless flight,
And age is sure to follow youth
as day comes after night,
And once again it's proven
that the restless brain of man
Is powerless to alter God's great, unchanging plan. . .
But while our steps grow slower
and we grow more tired, too,
The soul goes roaring upward
to realms untouched and new,
Where God's children live forever
in the beauty of His love.

Helen Steiner Rice

New Life

And in the resurrection
That takes place in nature's sod,
Let us understand more fully
The risen Son of God.
And let us see the beauty
And the glory and the grace
That surrounds us in the springtime
As the smiling of God's face.
And through a happy springtime
And a summer filled with love,
May we walk into the autumn
With our thoughts on God above:
The God who sends the winter
And wraps the earth in death
Will always send the springtime
With an awakening breath
To every flower and leaflet
And to every shrub and tree,
And that same God will also send
New life to you and me.

The Character
of God

Whoever does not love does not know God,
because God is love.

1 John 4:8 (NIV)

Helen Steiner Rice

God Is No Stranger

God is no stranger in a faraway place—
He's as close as the wind that blows 'cross my face.
It's true I can't see the wind as it blows,
But I feel it around me and my heart surely knows
That God's mighty hand can be felt everywhere,
For there's nothing on earth that is not in God's care.
The sky and the stars, the waves and the sea,
The dew on the grass, the leaves on a tree
Are constant reminders of God and His nearness
Proclaiming His presence with crystal-like clearness.
So how could I think God was far, far away
When I feel Him beside me every hour of the day?
And I've plenty of reasons to know God's my friend,
And this is one friendship that time cannot end.

The Hand of God Is Everywhere

It's true we have never looked on His face,
But His likeness shines forth from every place,
For the hand of God is everywhere
Along life's busy thoroughfare,
And His presence can be felt and seen
Right in the midst of our daily routine.
Things we touch and see and feel
Are what make God so very real.

⌘

Reflections of God's Face

⌘

The silent stars in timeless skies,
The wonderment in children's eyes,
The autumn haze, the breath of spring,
The chirping song the crickets sing,
A rosebud in a slender vase
Are all reflections of God's face.

Helen Steiner Rice

"In Him We Live and Move and Have Our Being"

We walk in a world that is strange and unknown,
And in the midst of the crowd we still feel alone.
We question our purpose, our part, and our place
In this vast land of mystery suspended in space.
We probe and explore and try hard to explain
The tumult of thoughts that our minds entertain,
But all of our problems and complex explanations
Of man's inner feelings and fears and frustrations
Still leave us engulfed in the mystery of life
With all of its struggles and suffering and strife,
Unable to fathom what tomorrow will bring—
But there is one truth to which we can cling. . .
For while life's a mystery man can't understand,
The great Giver of life is holding our hands,
And safe in His care there is no need for seeing,
"For in Him we live and move and have our being."

My God Is No Stranger

⤬

I've never seen God, but I know how I feel—
It's people like you who make Him so real.
My God is no stranger—He's so friendly each day,
And He doesn't ask me to weep when I pray.
It seems that I pass Him so often each day
In the faces of people I meet on my way.
He's the stars in the heavens, a smile on some face,
A leaf on a tree or a rose in a vase.
He's winter and autumn and summer and spring—
In short, God is every real, wonderful thing.
I wish I might meet Him much more than I do—
I wish that there were more people like you.

⤬

Helen Steiner Rice

God Is Never Beyond Our Reach

No one ever sought the Father
and found He was not there,
And no burden is too heavy to be lightened by a prayer.
No problem is too intricate, and no sorrow that we face
Is too deep and devastating to be softened by His grace.
No trials and tribulations are beyond what we can bear
If we share them with our Father
as we talk to Him in prayer. . .
And men of every color, every race, and every creed
Have but to seek the Father
in their deepest hour of need.
God asks for no credentials—
He accepts us with our flaws.
He is kind and understanding
and He welcomes us because
We are His erring children and He loves us, every one,
And He freely and completely
forgives all that we have done,
Asking only if we're ready to follow where He leads,
Content that in His wisdom
He will answer all our needs.

In Him We Live

A troubled world can find
Blessed reassurance
And enduring peace of mind,
For though we grow discouraged
In this world we're living in,
There is comfort just in knowing
God has triumphed over sin.
For our Savior's Resurrection
Was God's way of telling men
That in Christ we are eternal
And in Him we live again.

Helen Steiner Rice

His Likeness Shines Forth

In everything both great and small
We see the hand of God in all,
And every day, somewhere, someplace,
We see the likeness of His face.
For who can watch a new day's birth
Or touch the warm, life-giving earth
Or feel the softness of a breeze
Or look at skies through lacy trees
And say they've never seen His face
Or looked upon His throne of grace.
And man's search for God will end and begin
When he opens his heart to let Christ in.

God So Loved the World

Our Father up in heaven, long, long years ago,
Looked down in His great mercy
upon the earth below
And saw that folks were lonely
and lost in deep despair,
And so He said, "I'll send My Son
to walk among them there
So they can hear Him speaking
and feel His nearness, too,
And see the many miracles that faith alone can do.
For I know it will be easier to
believe and understand
If man can see and talk to Him
and touch His healing hand."
So whenever we have troubles
and we're overcome by cares,
We can take it all to Jesus, for He
understands our prayers.

Helen Steiner Rice

The Better You Know Him, the More You Love Him!

The better you know God, the better you feel,
For to learn more about Him and discover He's real
Can wholly, completely, and miraculously change,
Reshape and remake and then rearrange
Your mixed-up, miserable, and unhappy life
Adrift on the sea of sin-sickened strife—
But when you once know this Man of goodwill,
He will calm your life and say, "Peace, be still"...
So open your heart's door and let Christ come in
And He'll give you new life and free you from sin—
And there is no joy that can ever compare
With the joy of knowing you're in God's care.

ᴄ⌒ᴐ

The Power
of Love

And now these three remain: faith, hope and love.
But the greatest of these is love.

1 Corinthians 13:13 (NIV)

Helen Steiner Rice

A Pattern for Living

"Love one another as I have loved you"
May seem impossible to do,
But if you will try to trust and believe,
Great are the joys that you will receive.
For love makes us patient, understanding, and kind,
And we judge with our hearts and not with our minds,
For as soon as love enters the heart's open door,
The faults we once saw are not there anymore—
And the things that seem wrong begin to look right
When viewed in the softness of love's gentle light
For love works in ways that are wondrous and strange,
And there is nothing in life that love cannot change,
And all that God promised will someday come true
When you love one another the way He loved you.

Enfolded in His Love

The love of God surrounds us
Like the air we breathe around us—
As near as a heartbeat, as close as a prayer,
And whenever we need Him,
He'll always be there!

God Loves Us

We are all God's children
and He loves us, every one.
He freely and completely
forgives all that we have done,
Asking only if we're ready
to follow where He leads,
Content that in His wisdom
He will answer all our needs.

Helen Steiner Rice

What More Can You Ask?

God's love endures forever—
what a wonderful thing to know
When the tides of life run against you
and your spirit is downcast and low.
God's kindness is ever around you,
always ready to freely impart
Strength to your faltering spirit,
cheer to your lonely heart.
God's presence is ever beside you,
as near as the reach of your hand.
You have but to tell Him your troubles—
there is nothing He won't understand. . .
And knowing God's love is unfailing,
and His mercy unending and great,
You have but to trust in His promise—
God comes not too soon or too late. . .
So wait with a heart that is patient
for the goodness of God to prevail,
For never do prayers go unanswered,
and His mercy and love never fail.

He Loves You

It's amazing and incredible,
but it's as true as it can be—
God loves and understand us all,
and that means you and me.
His grace is all-sufficient for
both the young and old,
For the lonely and the timid,
for the brash and for the bold.
His love knows no exceptions,
so never feel excluded—
No matter who or what you are,
your name has been included. . .
And no matter what your past has been,
trust God to understand,
And no matter what your problem is,
just place it in His hand. . .
For in all our unloveliness
this great God loves us still—
He loved us since the world began,
and what's more, He always will!

Helen Steiner Rice

The Gift of Friendship

✄

Friendship is a priceless gift that
cannot be bought or sold
But its value is far greater than a
mountain made of gold—
For gold is cold and lifeless,
it can neither see nor hear,
And in the time of trouble it is powerless to cheer.
It has no ears to listen, no heart to understand,
It cannot bring you comfort
or reach out a helping hand—
So when you ask God for a gift,
be thankful if He sends
Not diamonds, pearls, or riches,
but the love of real true friends.

✄

The Joy of Giving

Each of you should give what you have decided
in your heart to give, not reluctantly or under
compulsion, for God loves a cheerful giver.

2 Corinthians 9:7 (NIV)

Helen Steiner Rice

A Gift of Love

~

Time is not measured by the years that you live
But by the deeds that you do and the joy that you give. . .
And from birthday to birthday, the good Lord above
Bestows on His children the gift of His love,
Asking us only to share it with others
By treating all people not as strangers but brothers. . .
And each day as it comes brings a chance to each one
To live to the fullest, leaving nothing undone
That would brighten the life or lighten the load
Of some weary traveler lost on life's road. . .
So what does it matter how long we may live
If as long as we live we unselfishly give.

~

The Blessing of Sharing

Only what we give away
Enriches us from day to day,
For not in getting but in giving
Is found the lasting joy of living,
For no one ever had a part
In sharing treasures of the heart
Who did not feel the impact of
The magic mystery of God's love.
Love alone can make us kind
And give us joy and peace of mind,
So live with joy unselfishly
And you'll be blessed abundantly.

Helen Steiner Rice

Heart Gifts

It's not the things that can be bought
That are life's richest treasures;
It's just the little "heart gifts"
That money cannot measure—
A cheerful smile, a friendly word,
A sympathetic nod,
All priceless little treasures
From the storehouse of our God—
They are the things that can't be bought
With silver or with gold,
For thoughtfulness and kindness
And love are never sold—
They are the priceless things in life
For which no one can pay,
And the giver finds rich recompense
In giving them away.

Make Me a Channel of Blessing Today

Make me a channel of blessing today—
I ask again and again when I pray.
Do I turn a deaf ear to the Master's voice
Or refuse to hear His direction and choice?
I only know at the end of the day
That I did so little to pay my way.

The Richest Gifts

The richest gifts
Are God's to give.
As long as you live,
May you walk with Him
And dwell in His love
As He sends you good gifts
From heaven above.

Helen Steiner Rice

Give Lavishly!
Live Abundantly!

The more you give, the more you get—
The more you laugh, the less you fret.
The more you do unselfishly,
The more you live abundantly—
The more of everything you share,
The more you'll always have to spare.
The more you love, the more you'll find
That life is good and friends are kind,
For only what we give away
Enriches us from day to day.

The Fragrance Remains

There's an old Chinese proverb
that if practiced each day
Would change the whole world in a wonderful way.
Its truth is so simple, it's easy to do,
And it works every time and successfully, too.
For you can't do a kindness without a reward—
Not in silver nor gold but in joy from the Lord.
You can't light a candle to show others the way
Without feeling the warmth of that bright little ray,
And you can't pluck a rose all fragrant with dew
Without part of its fragrance remaining with you.

Helen Steiner Rice

Faith to Meet Each Trial

From one day to another,
God will gladly give
To everyone who seeks Him
and tries each day to live
A little bit more closely
to God and to each other,
Seeing everyone who passes
as a neighbor, friend, or brother,
Not only joy and happiness
but the faith to meet each trial
Not with fear and trepidation
but with an inner smile.
For we know life's never measured by
how many years we live
But by the kindly things we do
and the happiness we give.

The Value of Prayer

The prayer of a righteous person
is powerful and effective.

James 5:16 (NIV)

Helen Steiner Rice

What Is Prayer?

Is it measured words that are memorized,
Forcefully said and dramatized,
Offered with pomp and with arrogant pride
In words unmatched to the feelings inside?
No, prayer is so often just words unspoken,
Whispered in tears by a heart that is broken,
For God is already deeply aware
Of the burdens we find too heavy to bear. . .
And all we need do is seek Him in prayer
And without a word He will help us to bear
Our trials and troubles, our sickness and sorrow
And show us the way to a brighter tomorrow.
There's no need at all for impressive prayer,
For the minute we seek God, He's already there.

The House of Prayer

Just close your eyes and open your heart
And feel your cares and worries depart.
Just yield yourself to the Father above
And let Him hold you secure in His love. . .
For life on earth grows more involved
With endless problems that can't be solved,
But God only asks us to do our best—
Then He will take over and finish the rest. . .
So when you are tired, discouraged, and blue,
There's always one door that is opened to you
And that is the door to the house of prayer,
And you'll find God waiting to meet you there. . .
And the house of prayer is no farther away
Than the quiet spot where you kneel and pray.
For the heart is a temple when God is there
As we place ourselves in His loving care. . .
And He hears every prayer and answers each one
When we pray in His name, "Thy will be done."
And the burdens that seemed too heavy to bear
Are lifted away on the wings of prayer.

Helen Steiner Rice

Wings of Prayer

On the wings of prayer our burdens take flight
And our load of care becomes bearably light,
And our heavy hearts are lifted above
To be healed by the balm of God's wondrous love,
And the tears in our eyes are dried by the hands
Of a loving Father who understands
All of our problems, our fears and despair,
When we take them to Him on the wings of prayer.

Begin Each Day by Kneeling to Pray

Start every day with a "good morning" prayer
And God will bless each thing you do
and keep you in His care. . .
And never, never sever the spirit's silken strand
That our Father up in heaven holds
in His mighty hand.

Thoughts of Peace

Whenever I am troubled and lost in deep despair
I bundle all my troubles up
and go to God in prayer. . .
I tell Him I am heartsick and lost and lonely, too,
That my heart is deeply burdened
and I don't know what to do. . .
But I know He stilled the tempest
and calmed the angry sea,
And I humbly ask if in His love
He'll do the same for me. . .
And then I just keep quiet
and think only thoughts of peace,
And if I abide in stillness
my restless murmurings cease.

Helen Steiner Rice

Talk It Over with God

You're worried and troubled about everything,
Wondering and fearing what tomorrow will bring.
You long to tell someone, for you feel so alone,
But your friends are all burdened
with cares of their own.
There is only one place and only one friend
Who is never too busy, and you can always depend
On Him to be waiting with arms open wide
To hear all the troubles you came to confide. . .
For the heavenly Father will always be there
When you seek Him and find Him
at the altar of prayer.

No Prayer Goes Unheard

Often we pause and wonder
when we kneel down and pray,
Can God really hear the prayers that we say?
But if we keep praying and talking to Him,
He'll brighten the soul that was clouded and dim,
And as we continue, our burden seems lighter,
Our sorrow is softened, and our outlook is brighter.
For though we feel helpless
and alone when we start,
A prayer is the key that opens the heart,
And as the heart opens, the dear Lord comes in.
And the prayer that we felt we could never begin
Is so easy to say, for the Lord understands
And He gives us new strength
by the touch of His hands.

Helen Steiner Rice

Heart Song

There are so many, many times
God seems so far away
That I can't help but wonder
if He hears me when I pray.
Then I beseech Him earnestly
to hear my humble plea
And tell me how to serve Him
and to do it gallantly. . .
And so I pray this little prayer
and hope that He will show me
How I can bring more happiness
to all the folks who know me—
And give me hope and courage,
enough for every day,
And faith to light the darkness
when I stumble on my way,
And love and understanding,
enough to make me kind,
So I may judge all people
with my heart and not my mind.

God Already Knows

Beyond that which words can interpret
or theology can explain
The world feels a shower of refreshment
that falls like the gentle rain
On hearts that are parched with problems
and are searching to find the way
To somehow attract God's attention
through well-chosen words as they pray,
Not knowing that God in His wisdom
can sense all man's worry and woe,
For there is nothing man can conceal
that God does not already know. . .
So kneel in prayer in His presence
and you'll find no need to speak,
For softly in silent communion
God grants you the peace that you seek.

Helen Steiner Rice

He Understands

Although it sometimes seems to us
our prayers have not been heard,
God always knows our every need
without a single word,
And He will not forsake us
even though the way is steep,
For always He is near to us,
a tender watch to keep. . .
And in good time He will answer us,
and in His love He'll send
Greater things than we have asked
and blessings without end. . .
So though we do not understand
why trouble comes to man,
Can we not be contented
just to know it is God's plan?

Breakfast for the Soul

∾

I meet God in the morning
and go with Him through the day,
Then in the stillness of the night
before sleep comes I pray
That God will just take over
all the problems I couldn't solve,
And in the peacefulness of sleep
my cares will all dissolve.
So when I open up my eyes to greet another day,
I'll find myself renewed in strength
and there will open up a way
To meet what seemed impossible
for me to solve alone,
And once again I'll be assured
I am never on my own.

∾

Helen Steiner Rice

Now I Lay Me Down to Sleep

I remember so well this prayer I said
Each night as my mother tucked me in bed,
And today this same prayer is still the best way
To sign off with God at the end of the day
And to ask Him your soul to safely keep
As you wearily close your tired eyes in sleep,
Feeling content that the Father above
Will hold you secure in His great arms of love. . .
And having His promise that if ere you wake,
His angels reach down, your sweet soul to take,
Is perfect assurance that, awake or asleep,
God is always right there to tenderly keep
All of His children ever safe in His care,
For God's here and He's there
and He's everywhere. . .
So into His hands each night as I sleep,
I commend my soul for the dear Lord to keep,
Knowing that if my soul should take flight,
It will soar to the land where there is no night.

⌒

I Think of You and I Pray for You, Too

Often during a busy day
I pause for a minute to silently pray.
I mention the names of those I love
And treasured friends I am fondest of—
For it doesn't matter where we pray
If we honestly mean the words we say,
For God is always listening to hear
The prayers that are made by a heart that's sincere.

❦

The Power of Prayer

I am only a worker employed by the Lord,
And great is my gladness and rich my reward
If I can just spread the wonderful story
That God is the answer to eternal glory. . .
And only the people who read my poems
Can help me to reach more hearts and homes,
Bringing new hope and comfort and cheer,
Telling sad hearts there is nothing to fear,
And what greater joy could there be than to share
The love of God and the power of prayer.

Helen Steiner Rice

Helen Steiner Rice